Luscious Ladies

Adult Coloring Book

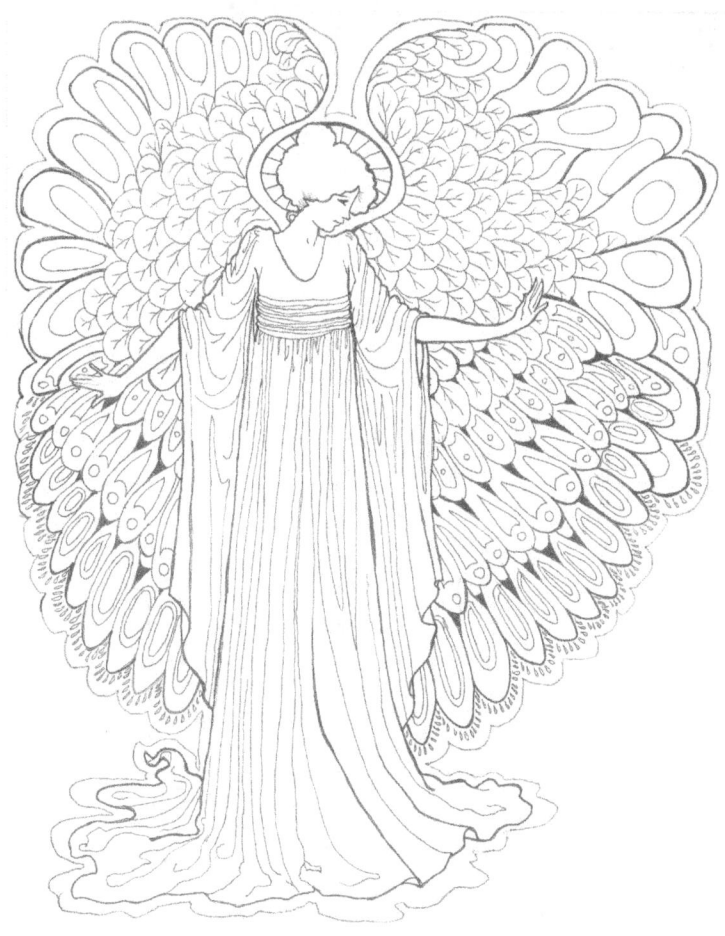

Betty Ann Fraley

INSTRUCTIONS

You will find in these pages areas of dark grey or black. If you are thinking this won't show color, don't worry. These dark values are there to help you enhance your color. Whatever color you choose will be darker and richer and save you time.

I prefer to use markers most of the time, but for the flesh tones, I work with pencils. Try both and see which you like best. Happy coloring!

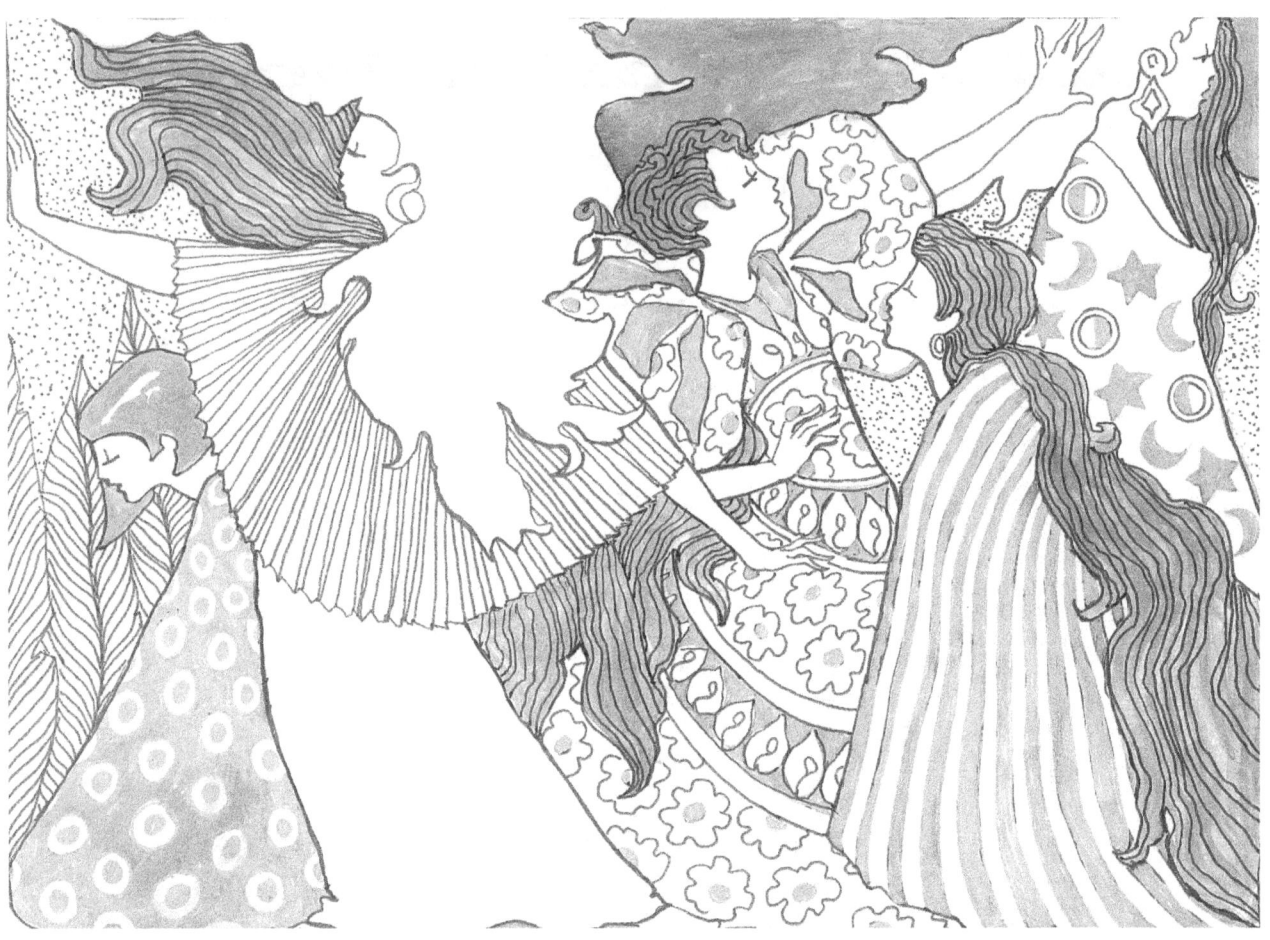

ISBN: 978-1533217547

Printed in the United States of America

Illume Writers & Artists
P.O. Box 86, Gilbertsville, New York, 13776
illumewritersartists@live.com

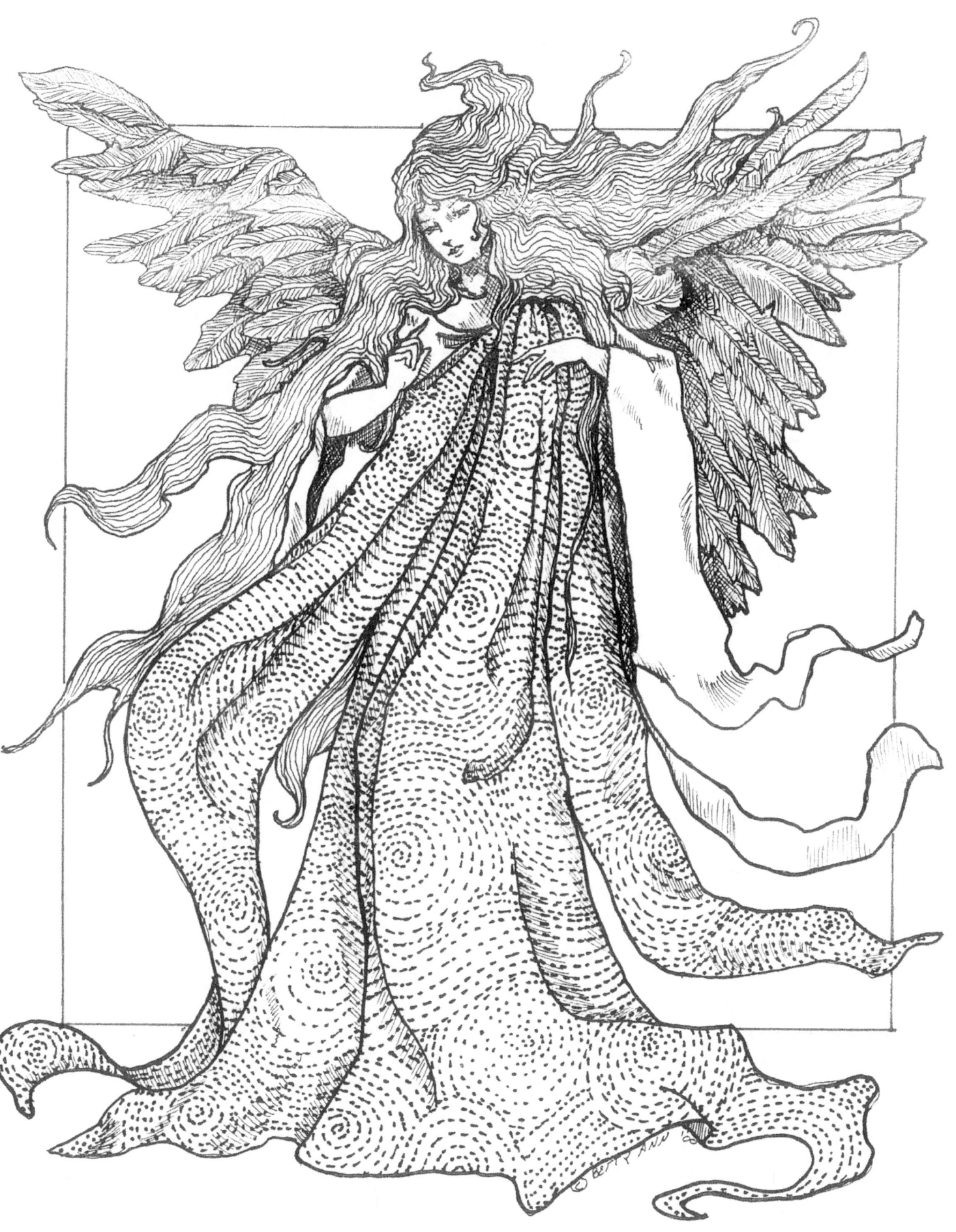

 **Cut out this page to use as backing, to prevent bleed-through to subsequent pages**

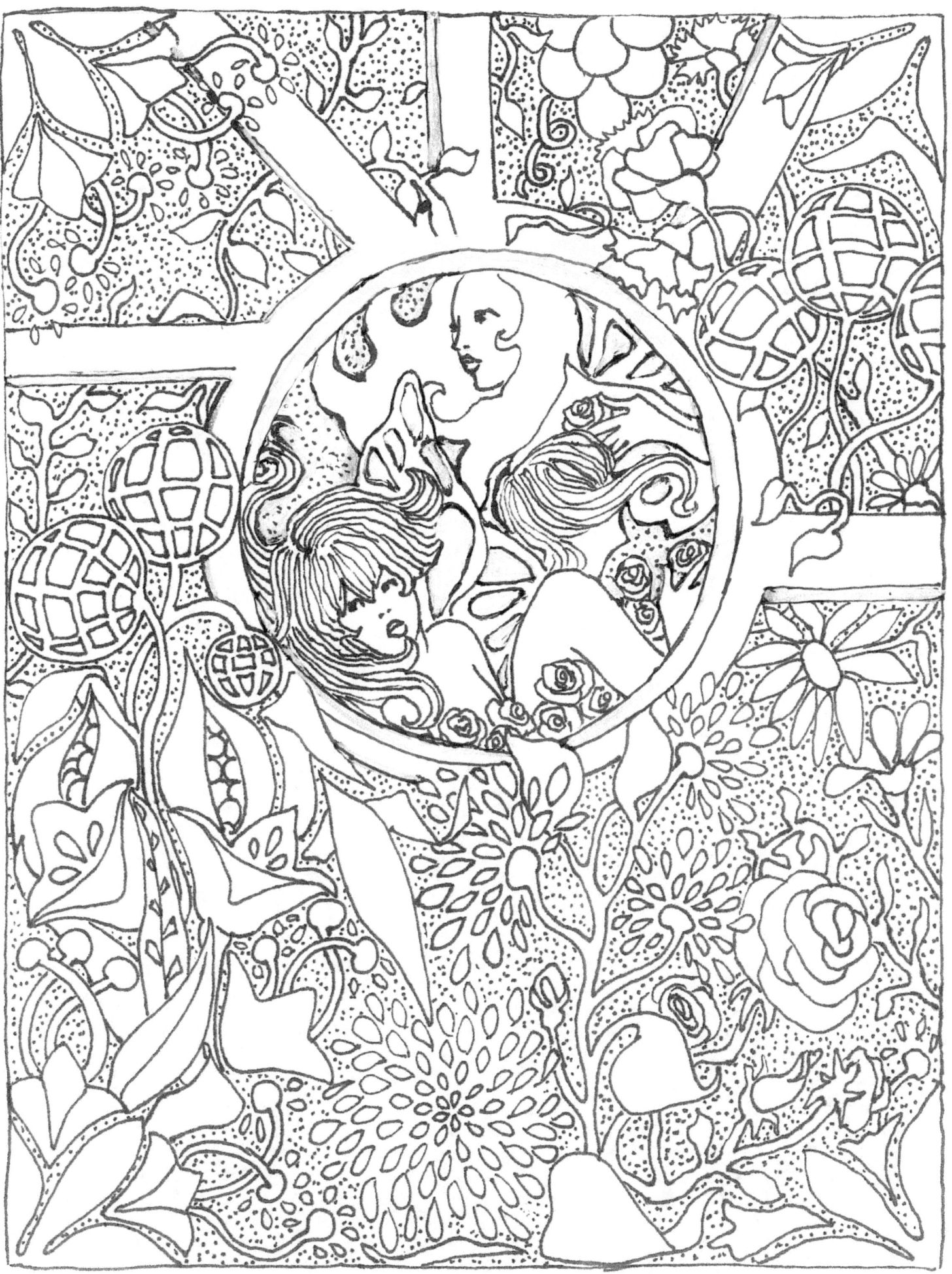

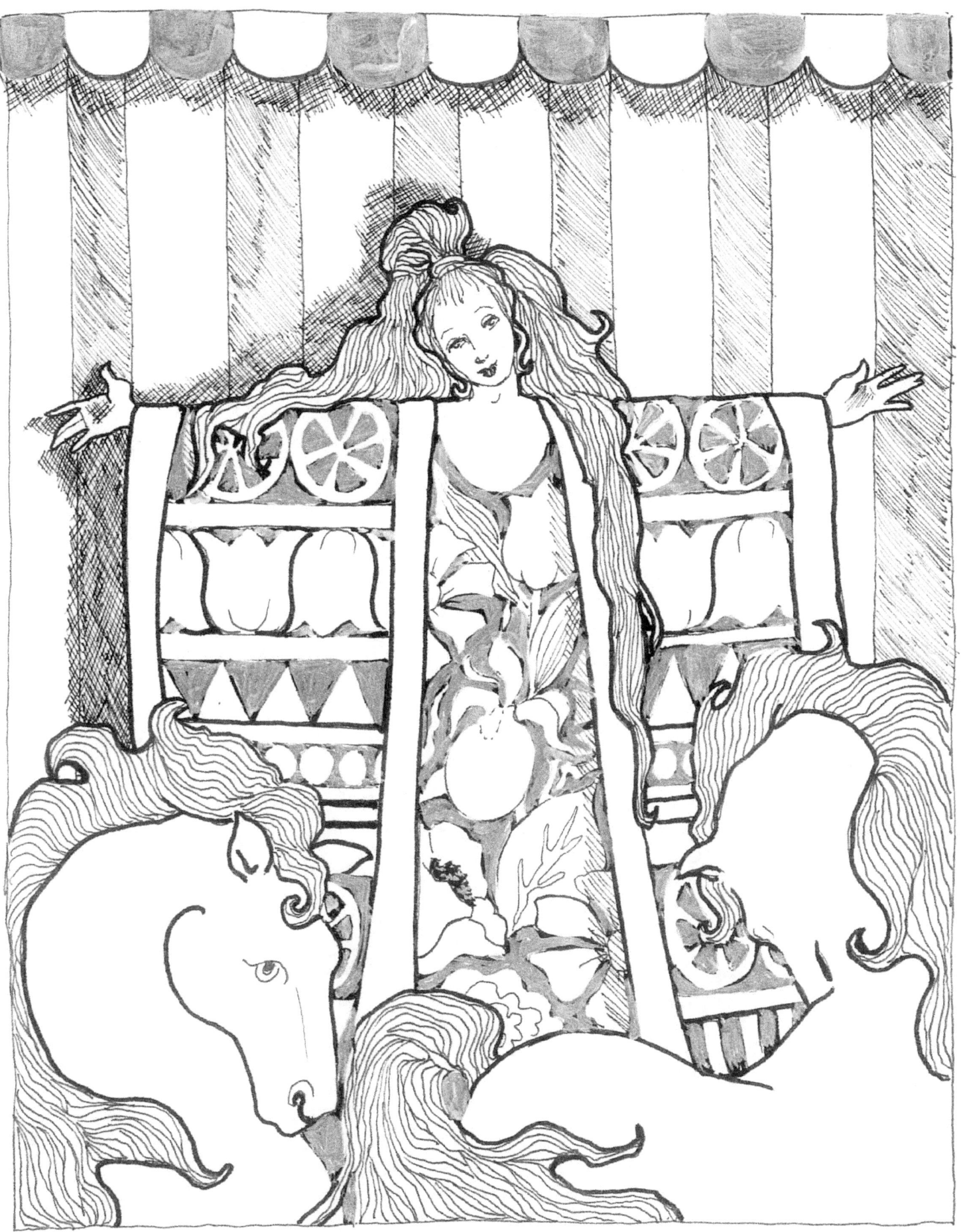

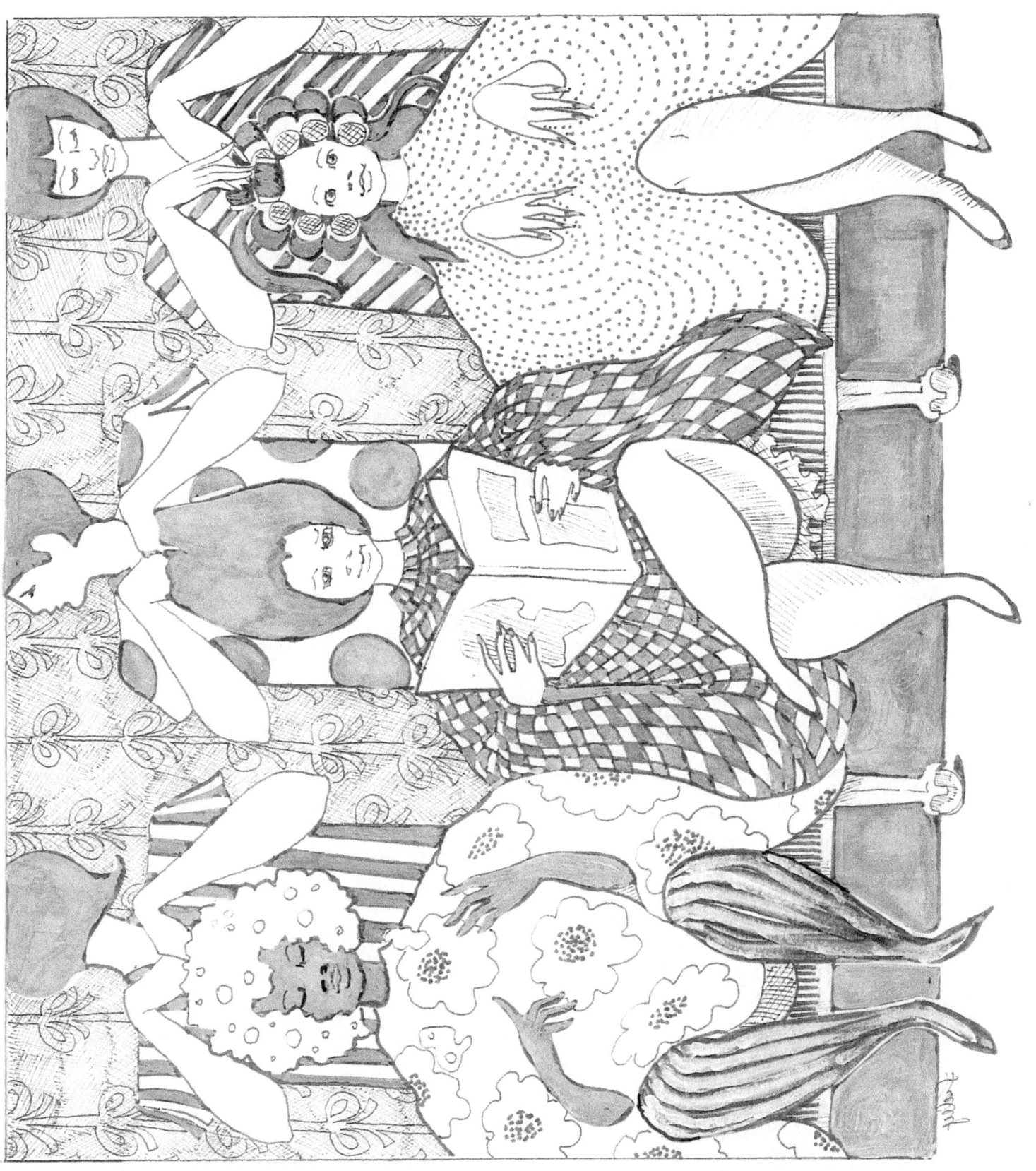

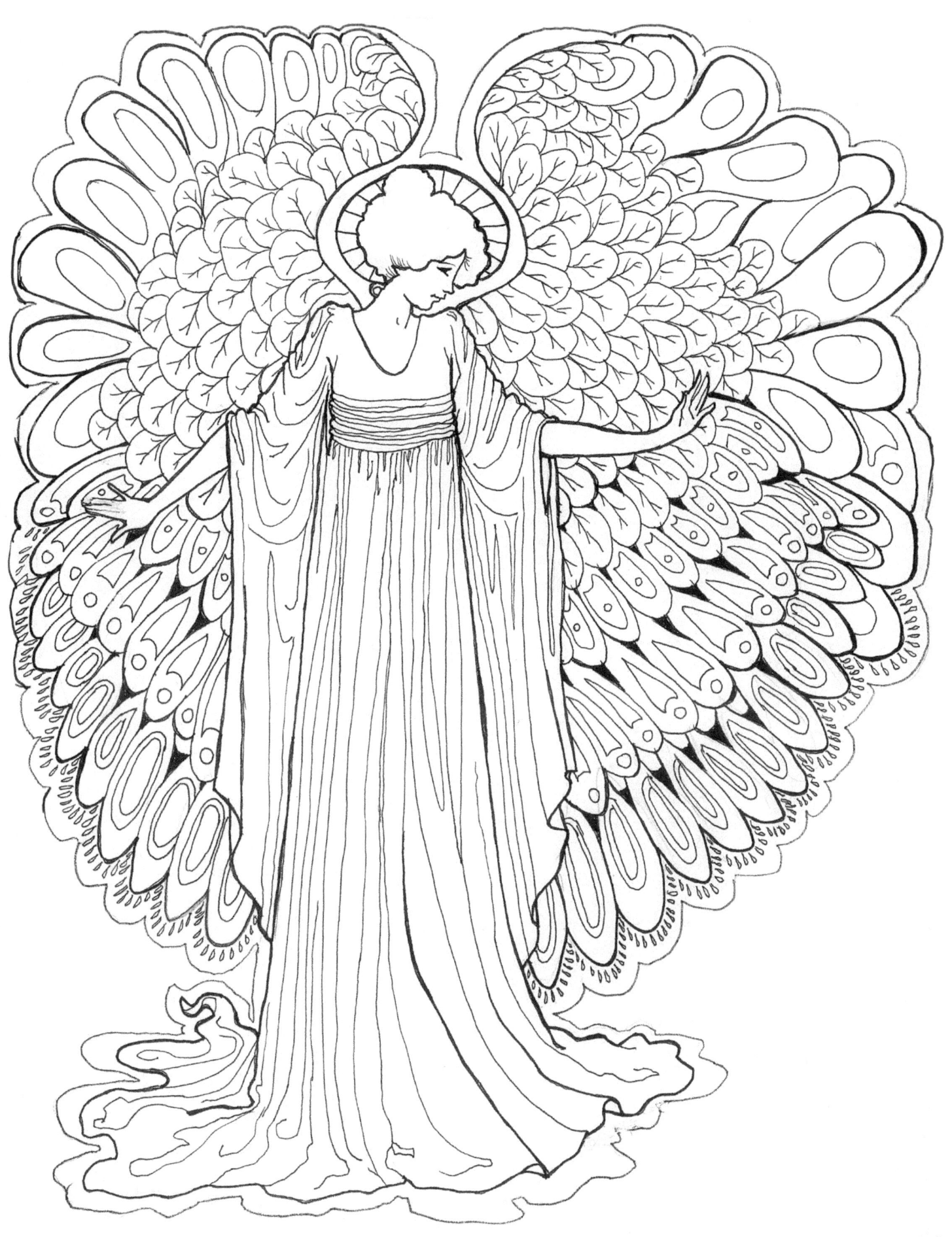

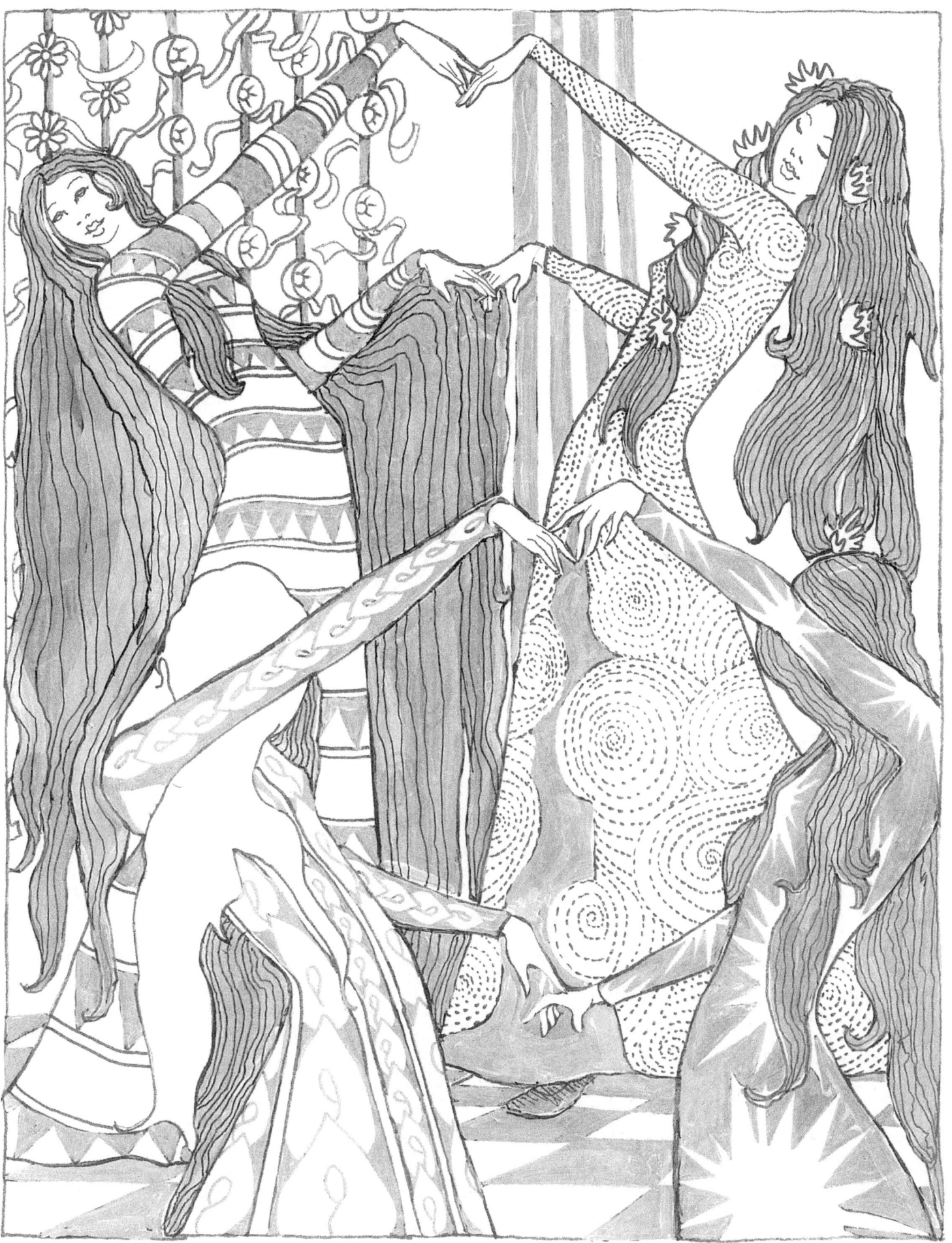

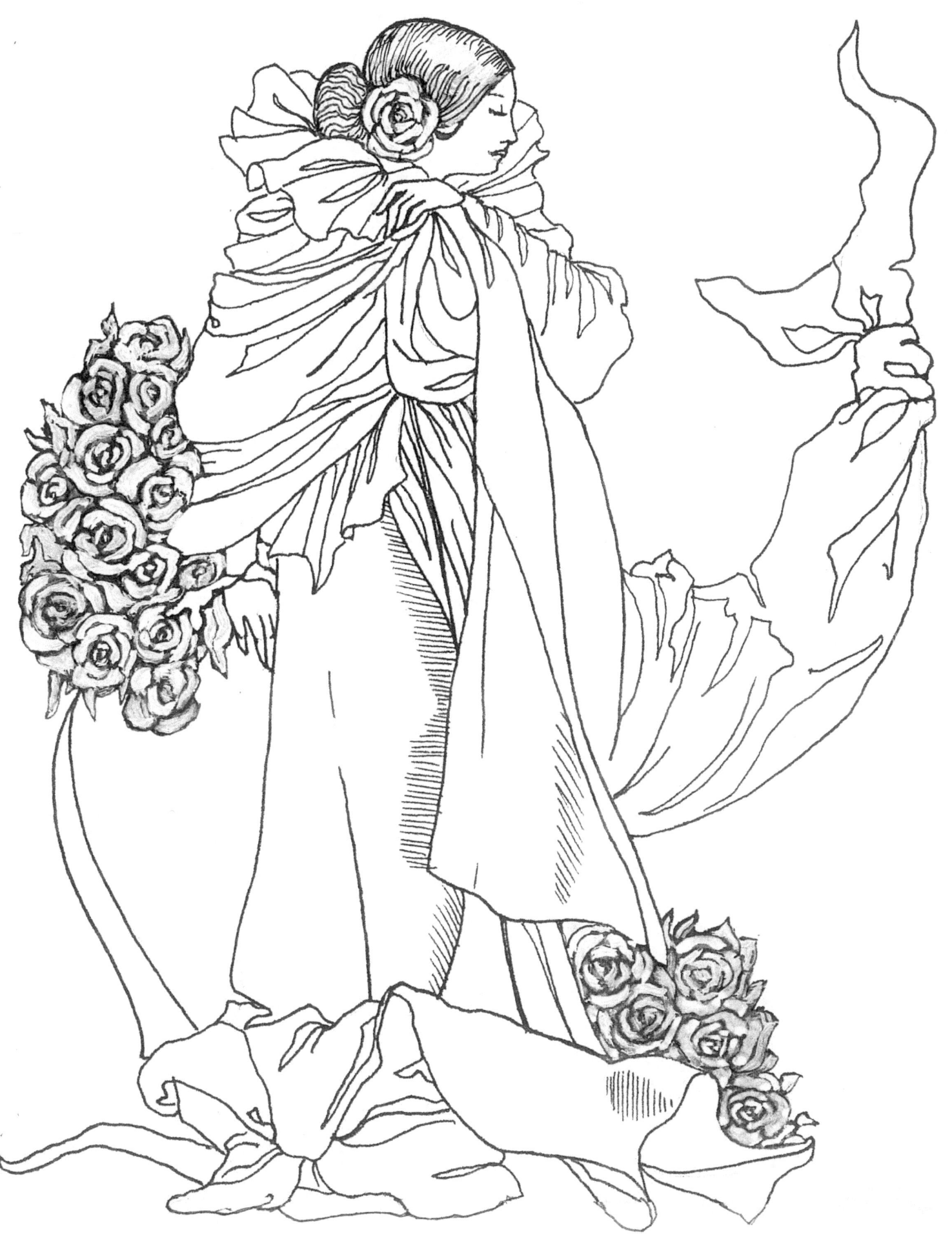

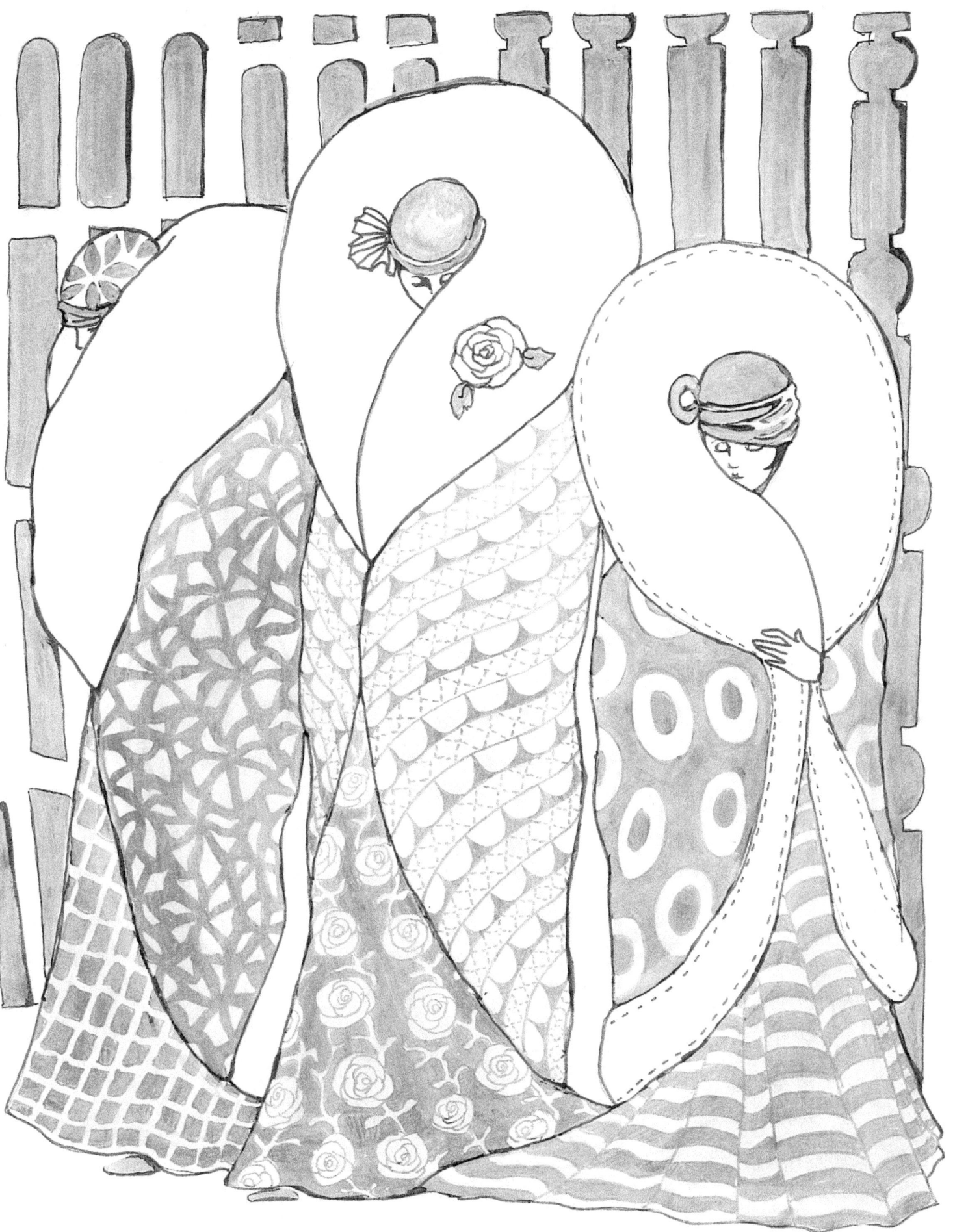

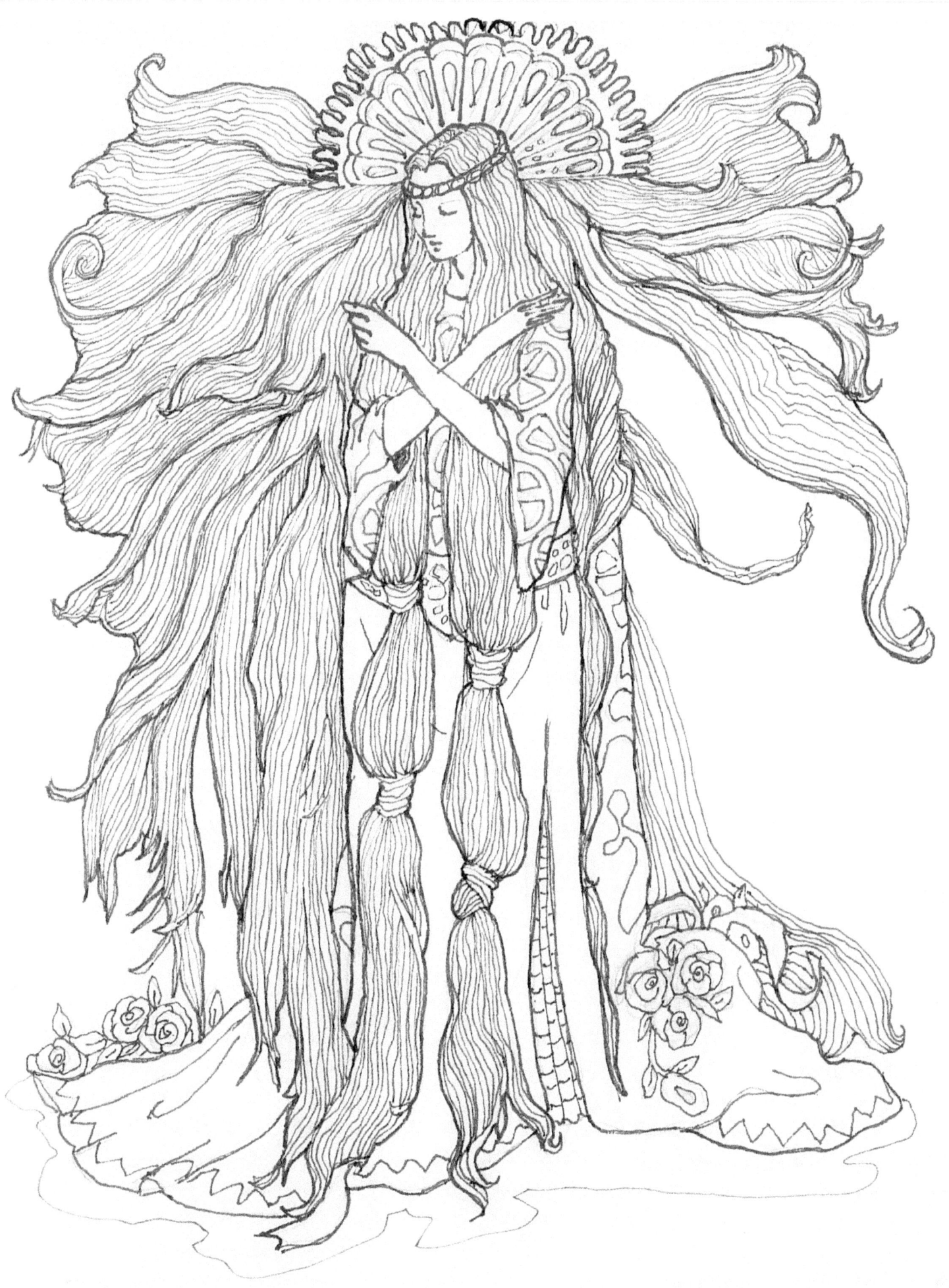

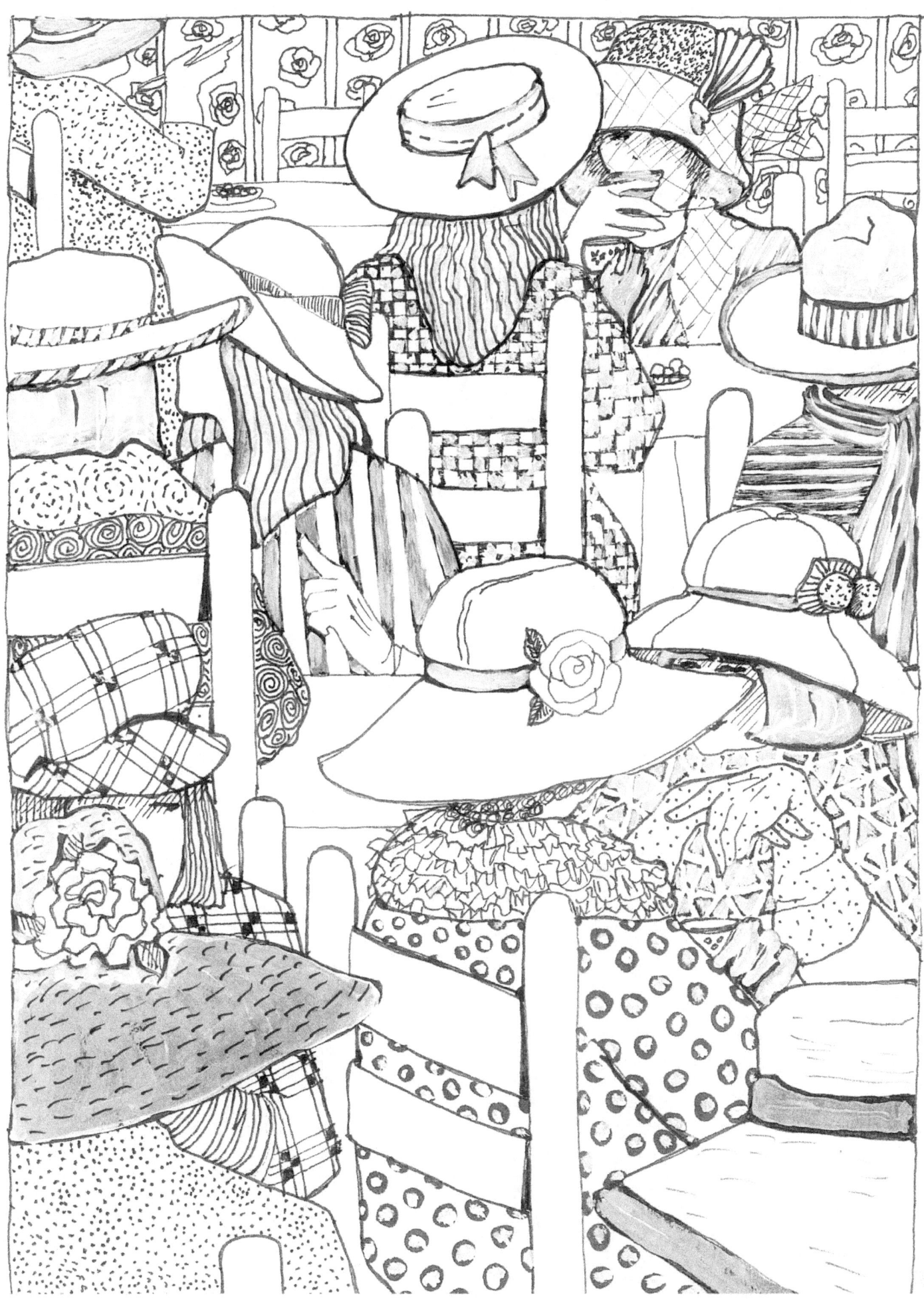

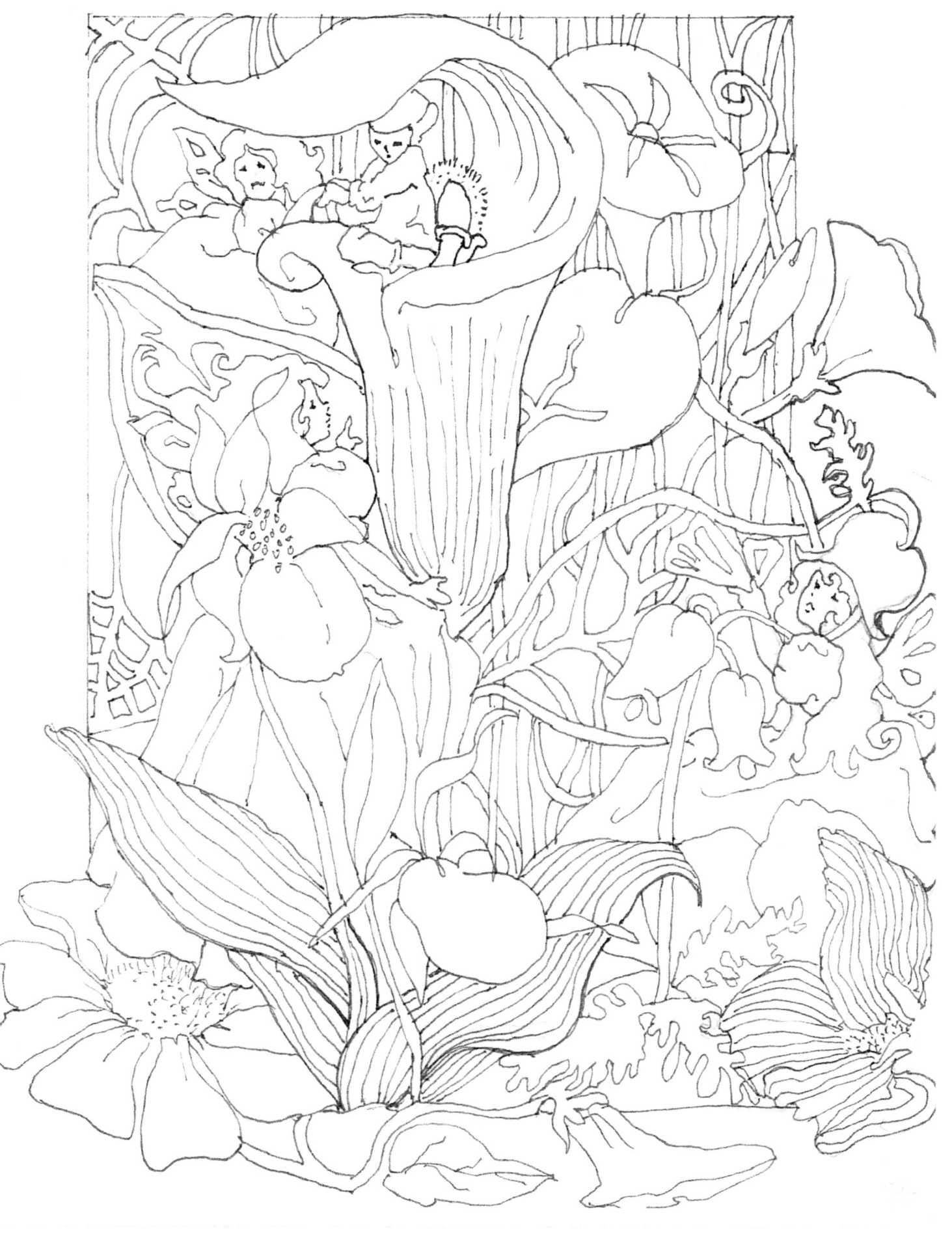

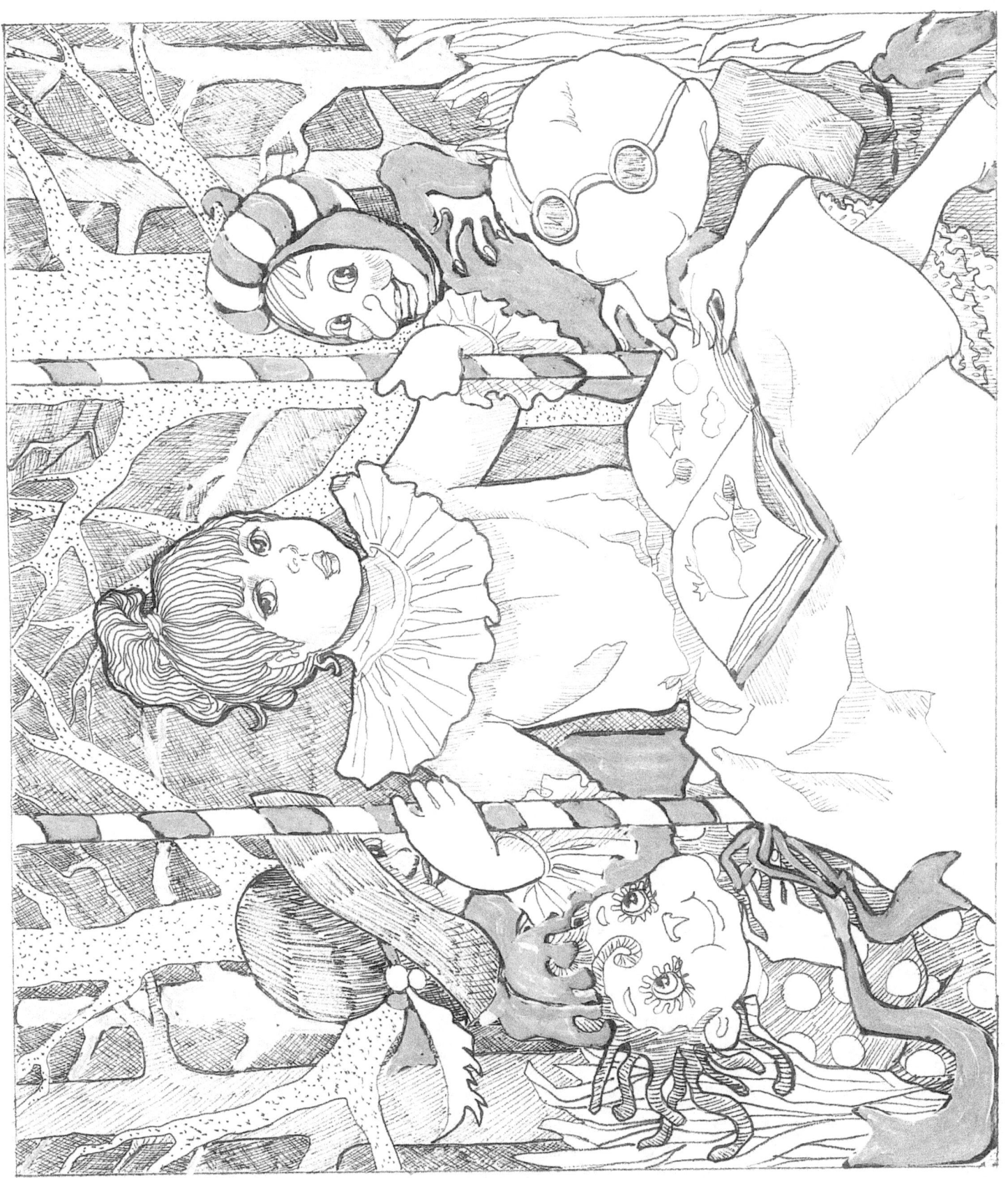

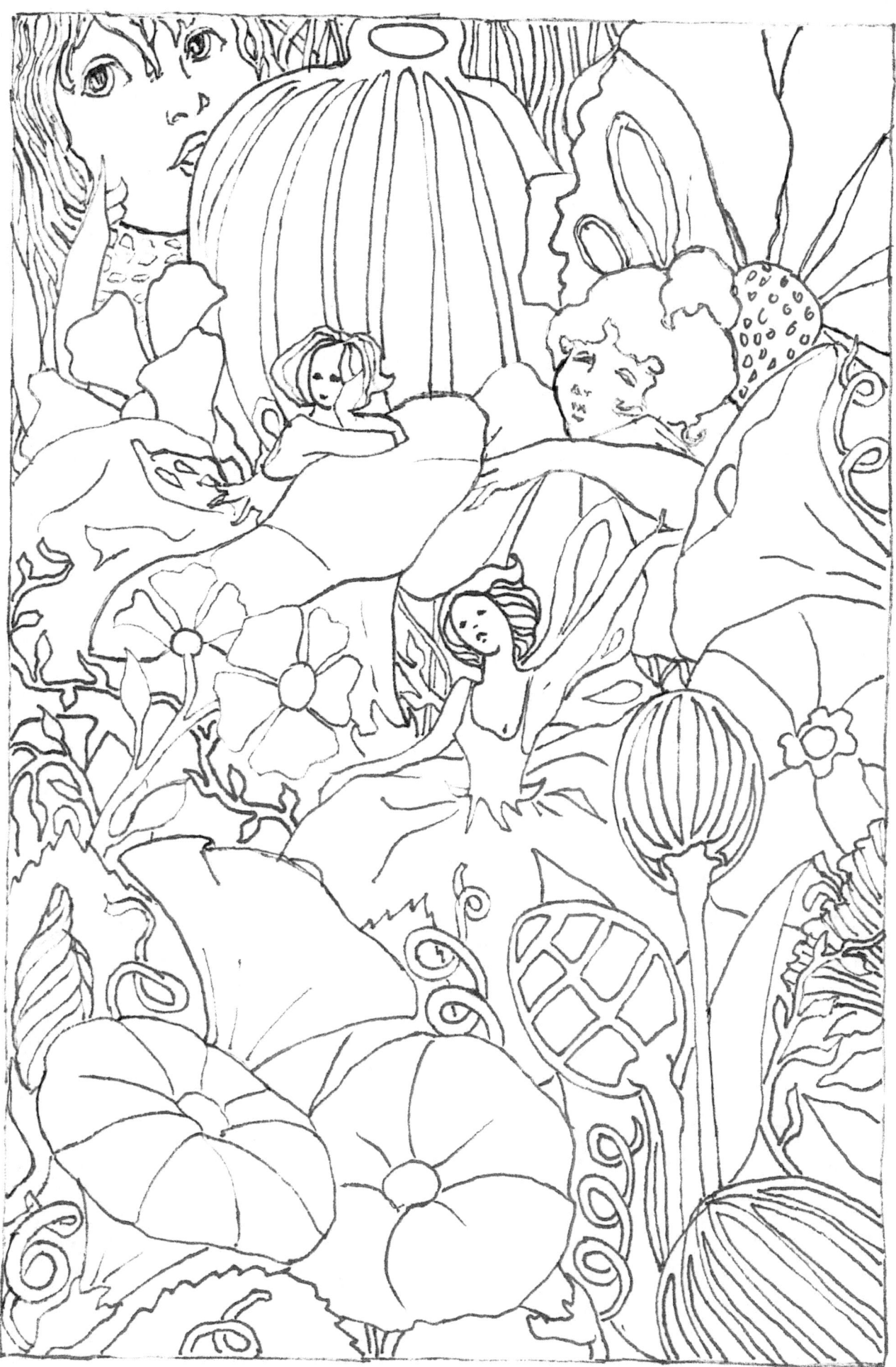

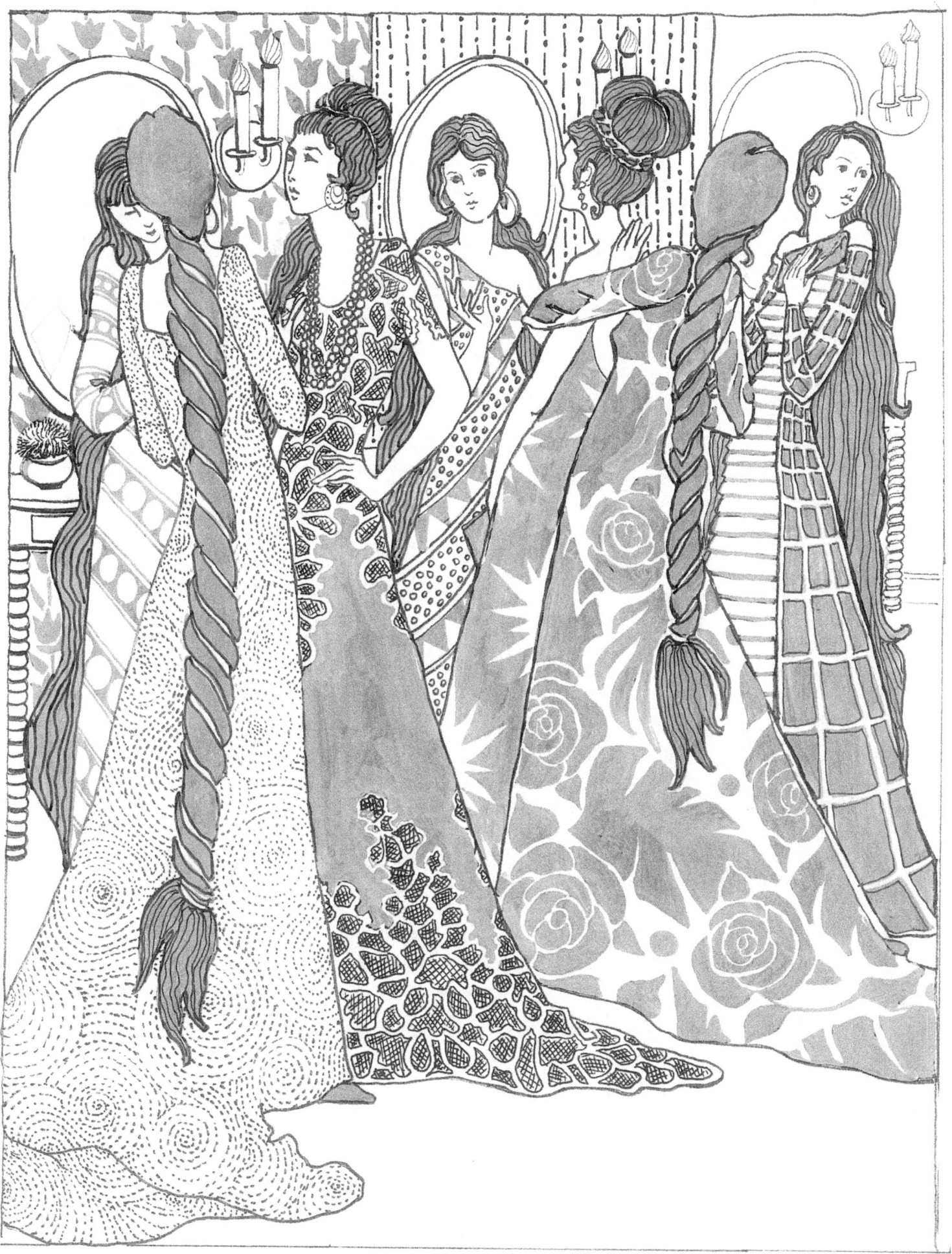

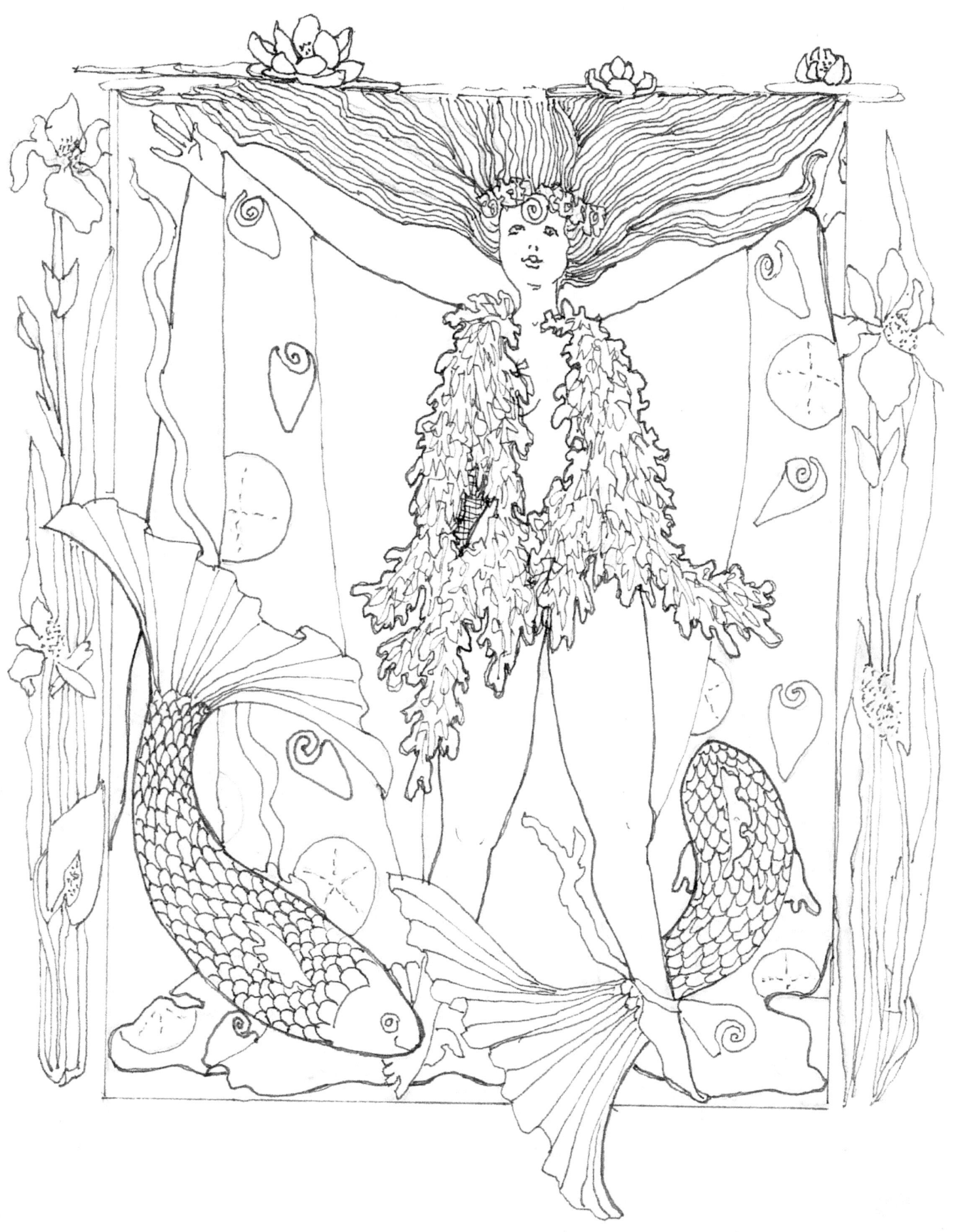

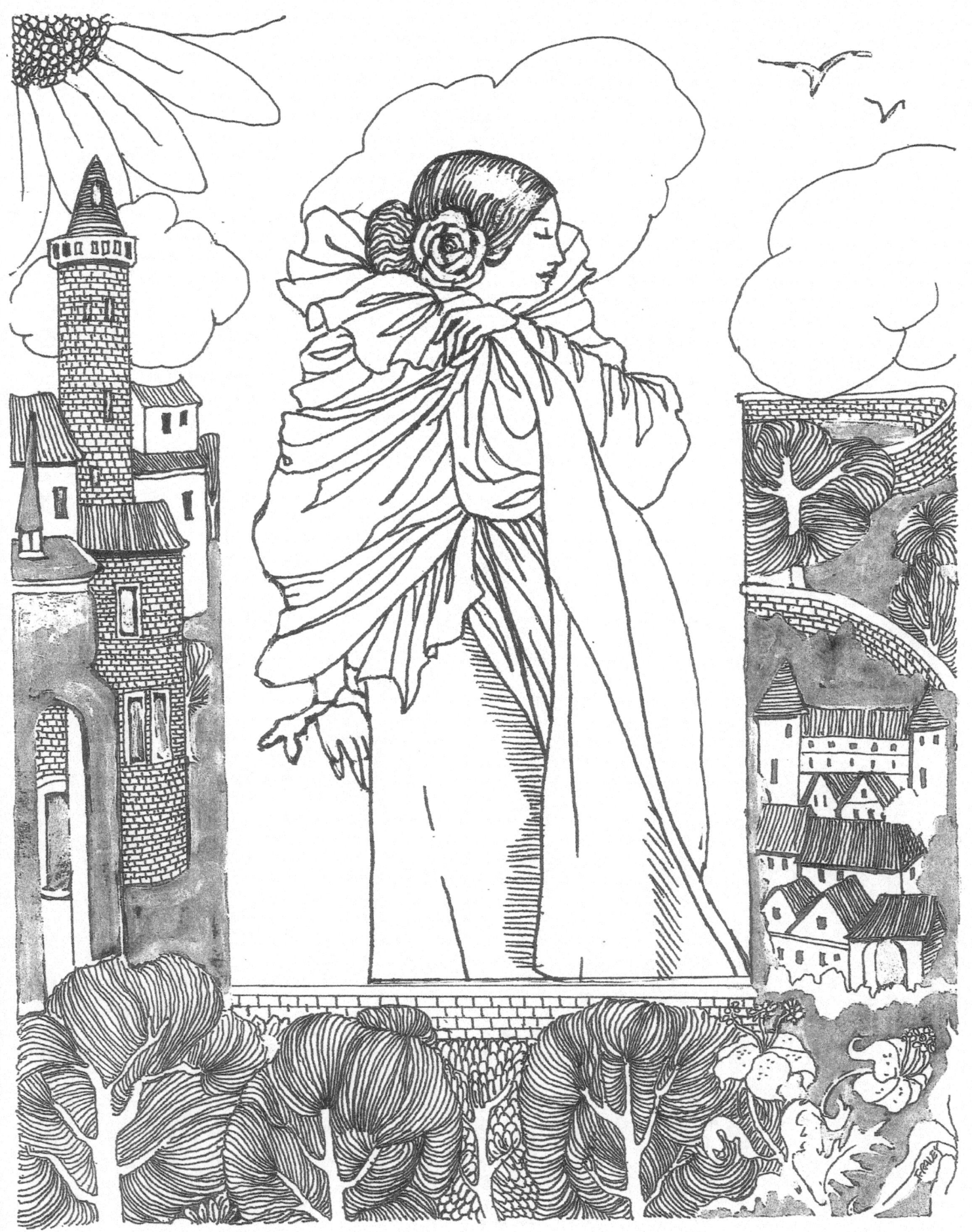

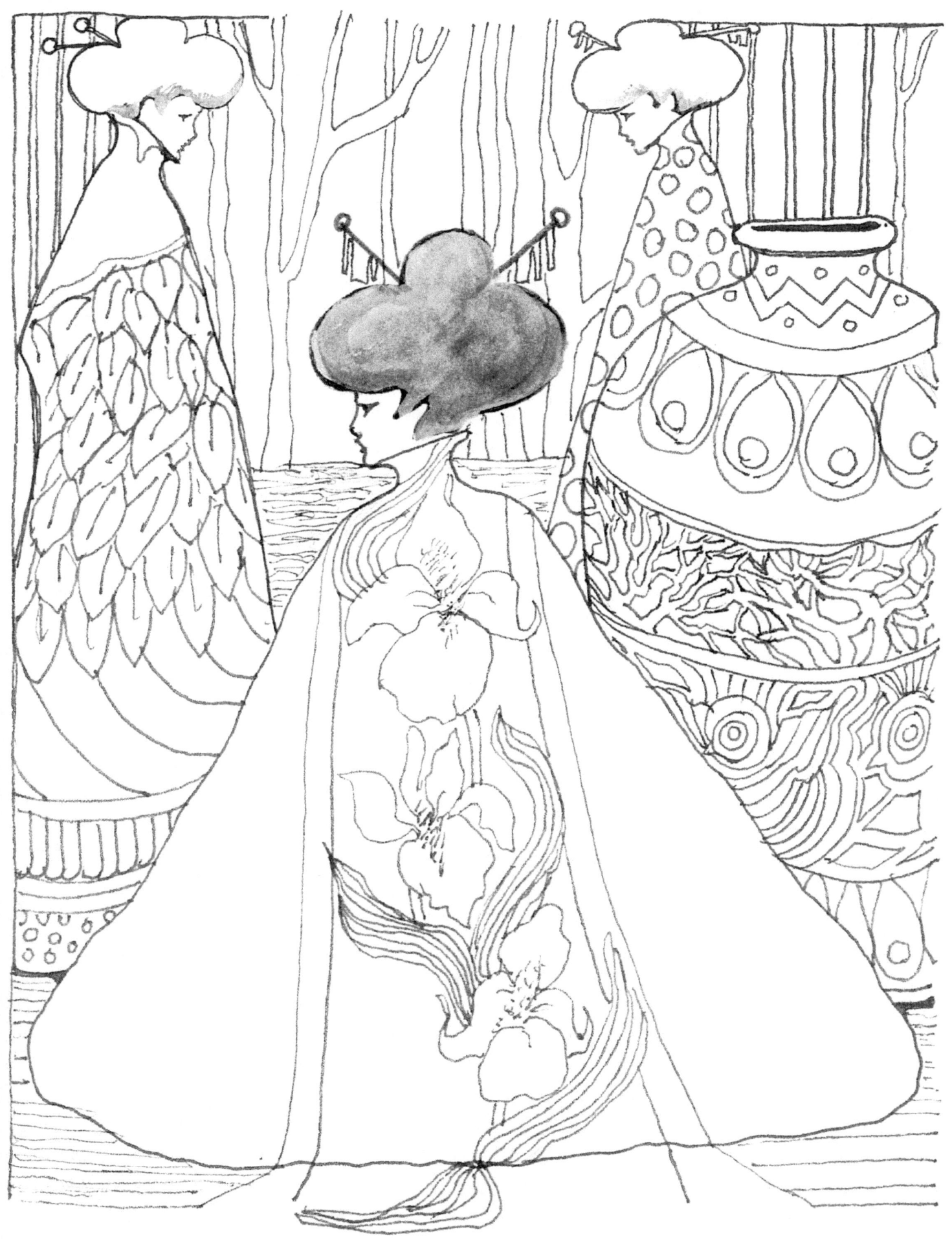

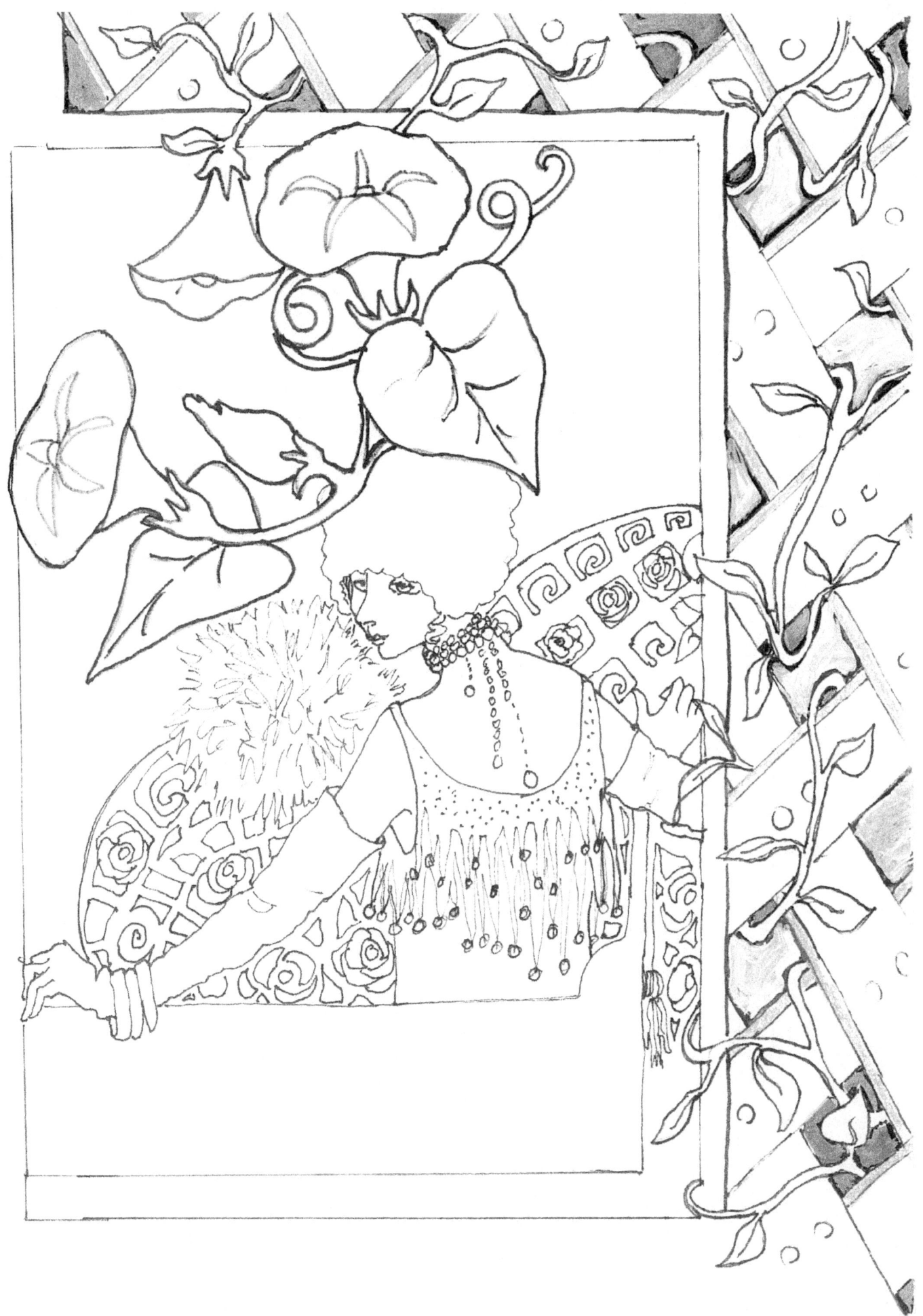

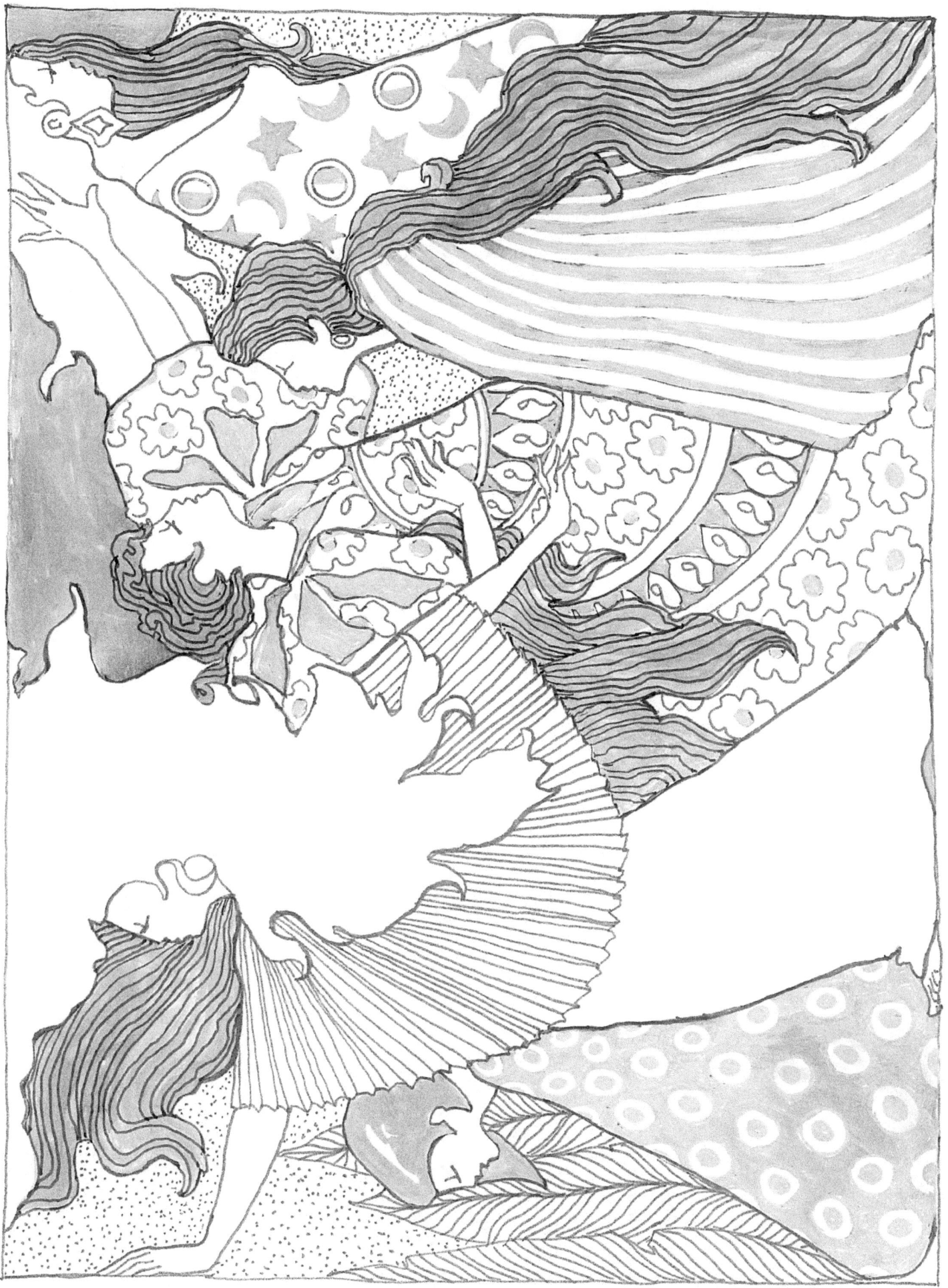

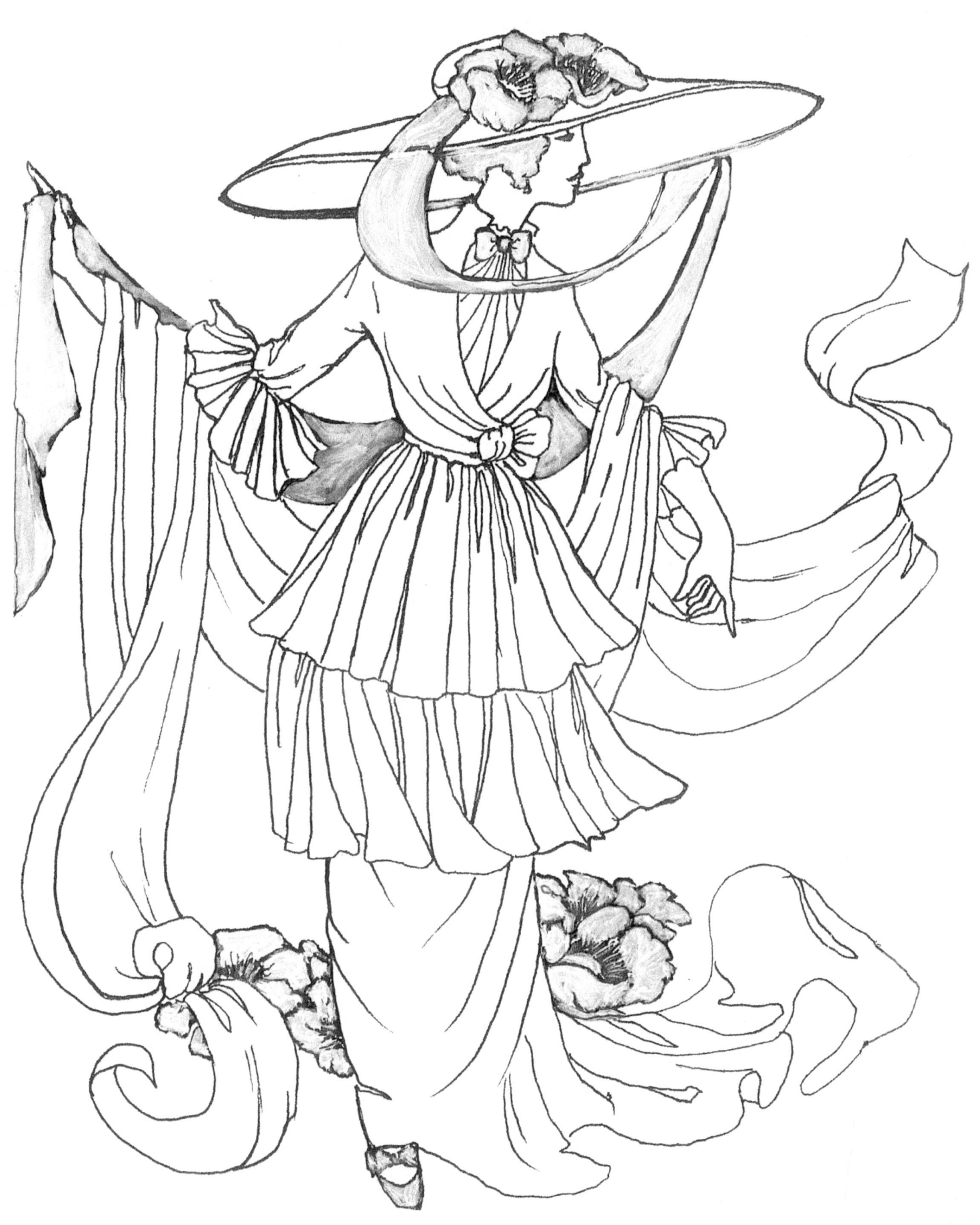

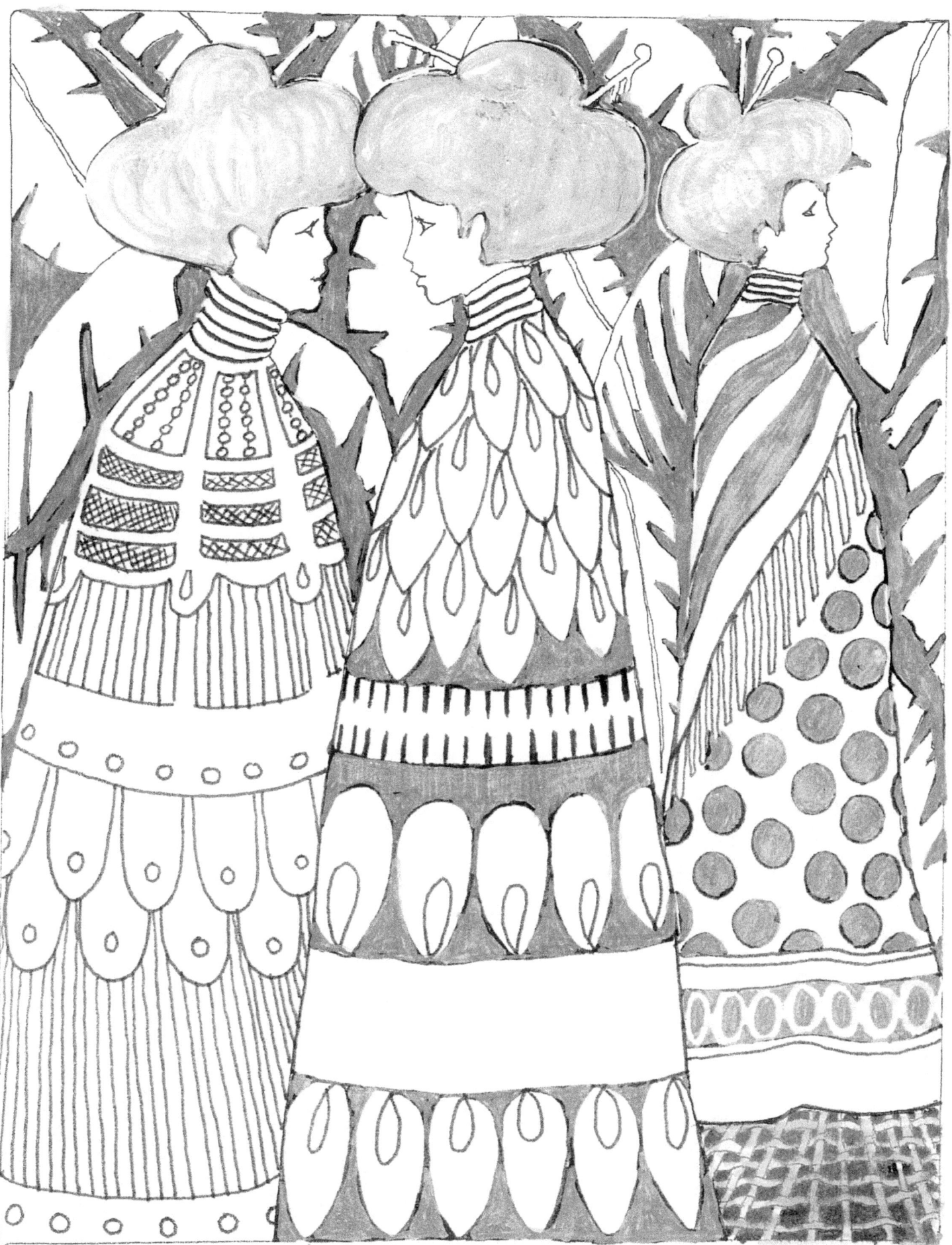

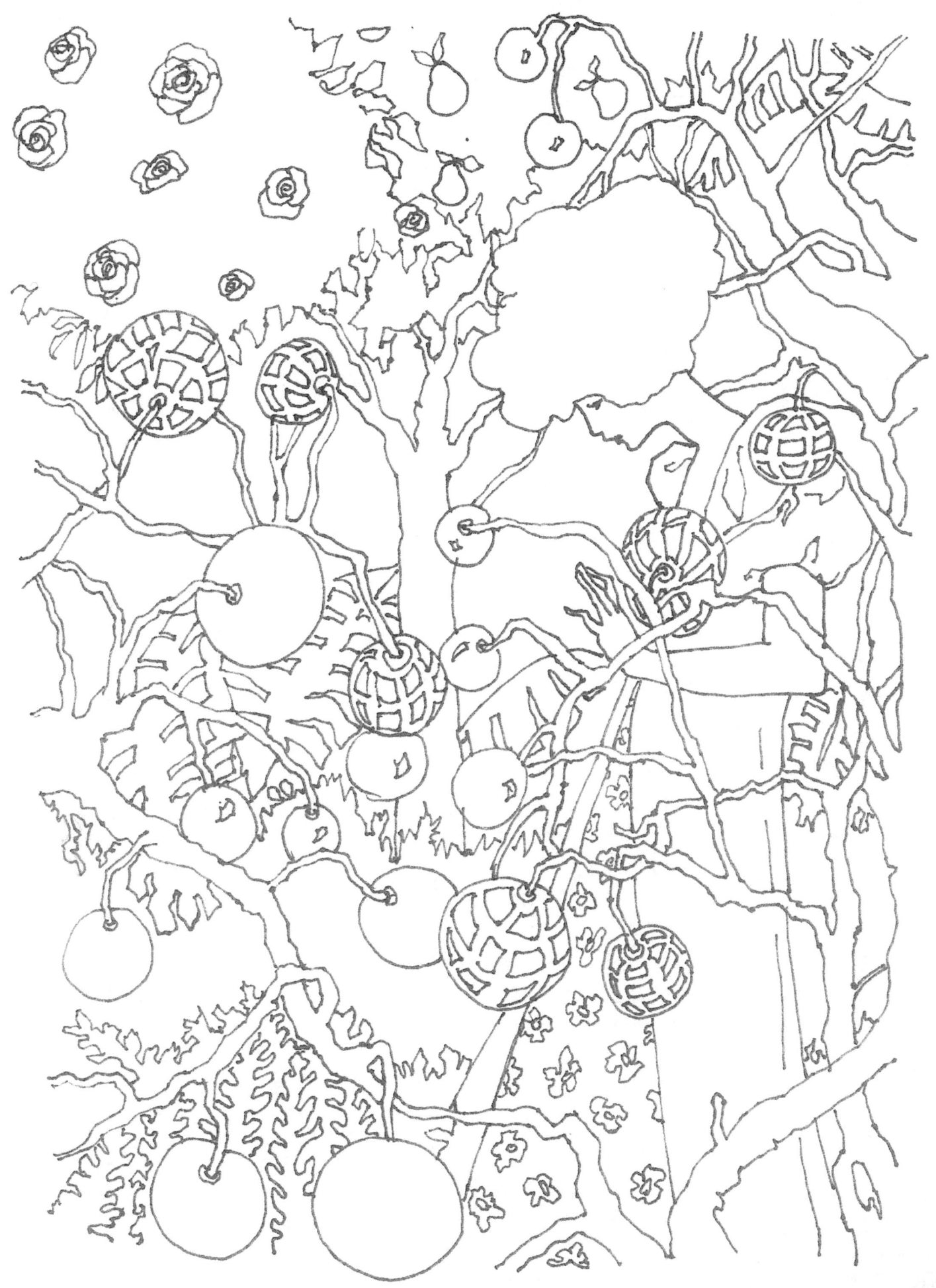